THE MAILBOX®
The Education Center®

Daily Reading Prompts

D0472555

782 Prompts to Use Throughout the Year

- ⦿ **Daily prompts for FICTION text**

- ⦿ **Daily prompts for NONFICTION text**

- ⦿ **Bonus prompts for BIOGRAPHIES**

- ⦿ **Reproducible reading tools**

Develops skillful readers and high-level thinkers!

Managing Editor: Hope Taylor Spencer

Editorial Team: Stephanie Affinito, Becky S. Andrews, Diane Badden, Jennifer Bragg, Kimberley Bruck, Karen A. Brudnak, Chris Curry, Juli Engel, Ann E. Fisher, Sarah Foreman, Tazmen Hansen, Marsha Heim, Lori Z. Henry, Krystle Short Jones, Debra Liverman, Kitty Lowrance, Barclay Marcell, Laura Mihalenko, Kim Minafo, Teri Nielsen, Jennifer Nunn, Mark Rainey, Hope Rodgers, Rebecca Saunders, Rachael Traylor, Sharon M. Tresino, Patricia Twohey, Zane Williard

www.themailbox.com

©2010 The Mailbox® Books
All rights reserved.
ISBN10 #1-56234-937-6 • ISBN13 #978-1-56234-937-0

Printed in the United States
10 9 8 7 6 5 4 3 2 1

HPS 211914

TABLE OF CONTENTS

WHAT'S INSIDE

366 Prompts for Fiction Text

366 Prompts for Nonfiction Text

50 Prompts for Biographies

Handy Prompt Symbols

August 13
- What do you think the main character might do next?
- ★ Why do you think the author wrote about this topic?

August 14

- Pretend you can travel to the setting of the story. Explain how you would go there and what you would do when you arrived.
- ★ What is the main idea of what you read today?

August 15
- Describe a choice the main character makes. Would you have made the same choice? Explain.
- ★ Would you like to read other books about this topic? Why or why not?

August 16
- Write a new title for the story. Explain why your title is better than the title the author wrote.
- ★ Are you satisfied with what you are learning? Explain.

Biography prompts on pages 100–103

AUGUST

BIOGRAPHY
- of anyone you know? Explain.
- earned about this person is...
- If you could meet this person, what would you ask him or her? Why?
- Which fact about this person has surprised you the most? Why?
- Would you like to have lunch with this person? Why or why not?
- I think the person I read about today would like to read...
- I think my teacher would be surprised to learn that the person I am reading about...
- Pretend that you are the person you are reading about. Use your senses to describe the place where you live.
- What does the author do to make this text more interesting? Explain.
- How does this person show kindness to others? Explain.
- Is this person strong? Why or why not?
- Describe one problem this person had. What did the person do? Would you have done the same thing? Why or why not?
- Would you want to be friends with this person? Why or why not?

Name _____
Title _____
Author _____

Book Review
Color the leaf in the matching column.

	Agree	Disagree
1. I enjoyed this book.	🍃	🍃
2. I thought the problem was interesting.	🍃	🍃
3. I would have solved the problem the way the author did.	🍃	🍃
4. I would read another book by this author.	🍃	🍃
5. I liked the main character.	🍃	🍃
6. I would like to meet the main character.	🍃	🍃
7. I would read more books about this character.	🍃	🍃
8. I would like to visit the story's setting.	🍃	🍃

Comments
_____
_____
_____

Plus Reproducible Reading Tools

107

August 1

● Today my reading reminded me…   ★ Today I learned…

August 2

● Think about the setting. Describe some smells you might smell.

★ I did not know…

August 3

● August is National Inventors' Month. Draw or describe an invention the main character can use. Explain how it works.

★ Describe a picture from your reading. Tell how it helped you understand the topic.

August 4

● Did you read about an important story event today? Explain.

★ What fact surprised you the most? Why?

Daily Reading Prompts • ©The Mailbox® Books • TEC61269

Biography prompts on pages 100–103

August 5

- Does the story take place in the summer? How do you know?

★ The more I learn...

August 6

- Describe the most important event that has happened in the story.

★ Write a fact from your reading. Tell how you will use this information.

August 7

- Use a Venn diagram to compare yourself to the main character.

★ I am wondering...

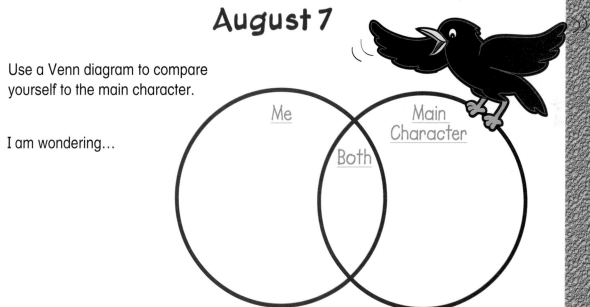

Me

Both

Main Character

August 8

- If you could talk to the main character, what advice would you give?

★ The most unusual thing I read today...

Biography prompts on pages 100–103

AUGUST

August 9

● Do you think the story takes place in the present? Why or why not?

★ If you want to be sure the information you are reading is true, how could you find out?

August 10

● Which character is the most unlike you? Describe the ways you are different.

★ What new word did you learn today? How will you use it?

August 11

● Who is telling the story? How do you know?

★ Write your opinion about what you read today.

August 12

● Do you think the story could happen in your neighborhood? Why or why not?

★ What two things did you know about your reading topic before you started reading?

Daily Reading Prompts • ©The Mailbox® Books • TEC61269

Biography prompts on pages 100–103

August 13

● What do you think the main character might do next?

★ Why do you think the author wrote about this topic?

August 14

● Pretend you can travel to the setting of the story. Explain how you would go there and what you would do when you arrived.

★ What is the main idea of what you read today?

August 15

● Describe a choice the main character makes. Would you have made the same choice? Explain.

★ Would you like to read other books about this topic? Why or why not?

August 16

● Write a new title for the story. Explain why your title is better than the title the author wrote.

★ Are you satisfied with what you are learning? Explain.

Biography prompts on pages 100–103

AUGUST

FICTION

NONFICTION

AUGUST

August 17

● Could your story take place on or near the beach? Why or why not?

★ Do you think the topic would be easier to understand if there were more pictures? What pictures would you include to make this topic easier to understand?

August 18

● The setting is important because...

★ Do you believe what you read today? Why?

August 19

● Do you want to read other stories by this author? Why or why not?

★ Do you think others would enjoy reading about this topic? Explain.

August 20

● Would this story make a good movie or TV show? Why?

★ Write three questions you can answer by using the information you read today.

Daily Reading Prompts • ©The Mailbox® Books • TEC61269

Biography prompts on pages 100–103

August 21

● List phrases that describe the setting.

★ Does your text have headings? Should it? Explain.

August 22

● How would the story be different if another character told it?

★ Before you started reading, did you think you would enjoy this topic? Were your feelings right? Explain.

August 23

● Write three events in the order in which they happened. Tell what may happen next.

★ Whom do you know that might like to read about this topic? Why?

Biography prompts on pages 100–103

FICTION ●

NONFICTION ★

AUGUST

August 24

● Describe the story's problem. How would you solve the problem?

★ Does the title make you want to read more? Why or why not?

August 25

● Which character do you trust most? Explain.

★ Write three details about your topic. Make a check mark next to the one that you think is the most interesting.

August 26

● Today is National Dog Day. In the United States, more people have dogs for pets than any other type of pet. What would be the best pet for the main character?

★ Sometimes I get sleepy when I read…

August 27

● Would you like to read a sequel to this story? Why or why not?

★ I now understand…

Biography prompts on pages 100–103

August 28

● Pretend you are a famous artist. Draw scenes from the story. Then write about your pictures.

★ Which details did the author put first, next, and last? Why do you think these details are ordered this way?

August 29

● Think about what you read today. Did one of the characters do something that you would do? Explain.

★ What have you heard other people say about this topic? Do they agree with the author?

August 30

● Imagine that you are a news reporter. You are describing the setting of your story. Write your news story.

★ I think the author might be wrong about...

August 31

● This story would be different if...

★ Was the information you read today easy to understand? Why or why not?

A U G U S T

Biography prompts on pages 100–103

September 1

- ● When I was reading today, I was reminded of the time…

- ★ What information is the most interesting to you?

September 2

- ● Do you wish you were like any of the characters? Explain.

- ★ One thing this author does well…

September 3

- ● How is the setting of the story different from where you live?

- ★ What is something you learned that you want to remember? Why?

September 4

- ● What do you think might happen next? Why?

- ★ List two facts from your reading today. Tell how they are alike and how they are different.

Daily Reading Prompts • ©The Mailbox® Books • TEC61269

Biography prompts on pages 100–103

September 5

● Name two reasons you do or do not like the main character. Explain your answer by giving examples of the character's actions.

★ Does this topic interest you? Why or why not?

September 6

● If I could change the events of the story, I would change…

★ Which facts in this text remind you of other facts?

September 7

● September is Fall Hat Month. What type of hat would the main character wear? Why?

★ Do you think the author wrote this text to inform or persuade? Explain.

Biography prompts on pages 100–103

Daily Reading Prompts • ©The Mailbox® Books • TEC61269

FICTION ●

NONFICTION ★

S E P T E M B E R

September 8

● Would you recommend this story to a friend? Why or why not?

★ Would you spend your own money to buy another book on this topic? Why or why not?

September 9

● Is there a moral to this story? What is it?

★ What topic will you read about after you finish this book? Why?

September 10

● How has the main character changed from the beginning of the story? Explain.

★ I never knew…

September 11

● Five stars stands for the best story you have ever read. One star stands for a story you would never read again. How many stars would you give the story you are reading? Explain.

★ Do you think the author presents the topic fairly? Explain.

Daily Reading Prompts • ©The Mailbox® Books • TEC61269

Biography prompts on pages 100–103

September 12

● Today is Video Games Day. Would the main character in your story play video games? Why or why not?

★ When was this text written? Should the information be updated?

September 13

● Is the weather important to the story? Why or why not?

★ Is there anything about your text that makes it more interesting than you thought it would be? Explain.

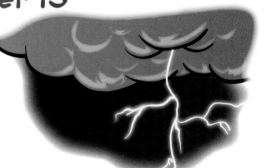

September 14

● When I read today, I thought about…

★ What was the most important part of what you read today? Explain.

September 15

● How would you summarize the main idea of the story?

★ Do you think the author has enough experience to write this text? Why or why not?

Biography prompts on pages 100–103

SEPTEMBER

September 16

● If you could change the end of the story, how would you change it?

★ Does the author tell what he or she did to research the topic? What else could he or she do to research the topic?

September 17

● How does the story make you feel? How does the author make you feel this way?

★ Was it easy to find information in the text? Which parts helped you find information?

September 18

● If you could be best friends with one of the characters, which one would you choose? Why?

★ Write a letter to a librarian explaining why this text should or should not be in the library.

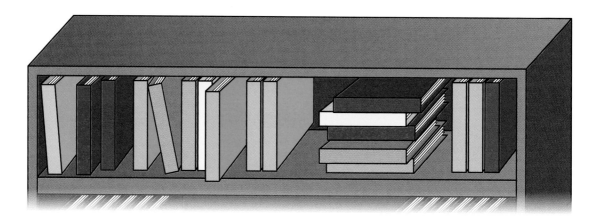

Daily Reading Prompts • ©The Mailbox® Books • TEC61269

Biography prompts on pages 100–103

September 19

● Does the main character show honesty? How do you know?

★ Is it important to learn about this topic? Why or why not?

September 20

● How does the story remind you of something in your life?

★ Were there any signal words, such as *first*, *next*, and *last*, that helped you understand the text you read today? Should the author use more of these words? Explain.

September 21

● Where else could the story take place? Explain.

★ Imagine that you will meet the author. What will you ask him or her?

September 22

● Is there anything you still want to know about the characters and their lives? Explain.

★ What information does the title give you?

Biography prompts on pages 100–103

FICTION

NONFICTION

September 23

● Autumn has begun. Does your story take place in autumn? How do you know?

★ If you were telling a friend about this text, what would you say? Why?

September 24

● List the words or phrases that make the story interesting. Explain each choice.

★ Write a letter to the author. Tell him or her whether you liked or disliked the text. Explain your opinion.

September 25

● Imagine that you could add a character to the story. Whom would you add? Why?

★ What events from your life help you understand the text? Explain.

September 26

● The events in this story…

★ How is the text organized? Would you have organized the text in another way? Why or why not?

Daily Reading Prompts • ©The Mailbox® Books • TEC61269

Biography prompts on pages 100–103

September 27

● If you could choose a pet for one of the characters, what would you choose? Why?

★ Does the author use any bold words to help the important information stand out? Should he or she? Explain.

September 28

● What is your favorite event from today's reading? Explain.

★ What questions did you have before you started reading? Did you find the answers as you read?

September 29

● Imagine you are one of the characters in the story. What do you see, hear, and feel?

★ If you could rewrite part of this book, which part would you rewrite? Why?

September 30

● Do you think the plot is a good one? Why or why not?

★ Why did you choose to read this text? Would you want to read more on this topic?

Biography prompts on pages 100–103

SEPTEMBER

October 1

● Imagine your teacher has asked you to make labels for book baskets. What label would you put on the basket for this story? Why?

★ October is National Book Month. Imagine you have been asked to make a speech about what you're reading. What will you say?

Historical Fiction

October 2

● Would you like to be one of the characters in the story? Why or why not?

★ Does your text have a map in it? Should it? Why or why not?

October 3

● Does a character tell the story? How do you know?

★ Right now, the most important thing about this topic is…

October 4

Events

1. _____
   _____
2. _____
   _____

● Write to describe the events in your story. What do you think will happen next? Why?

★ Would an expert agree with everything in this text? Why or why not?

Daily Reading Prompts • ©The Mailbox® Books • TEC61269

Biography prompts on pages 100–103

October 5

● How would you change one of the characters if you could? Why?

★ One thing I learned today that a friend would want to know is...

October 6

● How would you change the cover of the story? Why?

★ Find an interesting sentence and copy it. Why is it interesting?

October 7

● The author asks you to choose a different setting for the story. What will you choose? Why?

★ If your text could talk, what would it say?

October 8

● A quote is something someone says. Find your favorite quote from this story. Explain why you chose it.

★ In October, people celebrate Eat Better, Eat Together Month. What kind of nonfiction book do you think this author could write about this month?

Biography prompts on pages 100–103

October 9

● What is the main character's problem? Have you or anyone you know ever had a problem like this? Explain.

★ If I were the author, I would have left out information about…

October 10

● Was there a word in the story that you did not understand? Did you use the story to help you learn the meaning of the word? Why or why not?

★ Would you read this text again? Why or why not?

October 11

● What do you think other characters would say about the main character? Why?

★ Choose one paragraph from the text. Write a question that can be answered by reading the paragraph. Repeat the activity with two more paragraphs.

October 12

● I hope the author will…

★ When I think about this topic, I am curious about…

Biography prompts on pages 100–103

October 13

● Do any of the characters remind you of someone you know? Explain.

★ Write five adjectives that describe your topic. Explain each choice.

October 14

● Would you rather live in the setting of the story or where you live now? Why?

★ Write a letter to a friend. Tell your friend what you've learned about the topic so far.

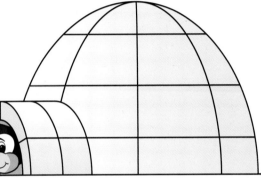

October 15

● What is something you may not find out until the end of the story?

★ Copy from the text one part that you have questions about. Write your questions.

October 16

● When I was done reading today, I felt…

★ Dictionary Day is today. Choose an interesting word from the text. Copy its meaning from the dictionary. Tell why you chose the word.

Biography prompts on pages 100–103

OCTOBER

October 17

● Pretend you are making a movie of the story. Which actor or actress will you choose to play the main character? Why?

★ Does the font make it easy for you to read the text? Why or why not?

October 18

● What do you think the author is trying to say about life? Explain.

★ The first interesting fact I learned while I was reading today was...

October 19

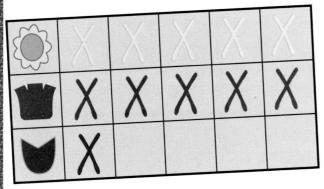

● Compare and contrast two main characters. Give two or more ways they are alike. Give two or more ways they are not alike.

★ Would a graph or diagram help you understand what you read today? Why or why not?

October 20

● Write a description of the main character. Use five or more adjectives in your description.

★ Look at one page of the text. If there were one thing you could change about the page, what would it be?

October 21

● Does the title of this story tell what the story is about? Explain.

★ What does the author want you to recall about the text you've read today? How do you know?

October 22

● List three things you learn at the start of the story.

★ What do you want your teacher to know about the topic you're reading about?

October 23

● Describe an event you read about today. Tell why it happened.

★ How did the headings and subheadings help you understand your reading today?

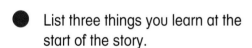

Biography prompts on pages 100–103

October 24

● Choose five words from the story. Replace them with words that are more descriptive. Explain each choice.

★ Would you tell a friend to read a book by this author? Why or why not?

October 25

● Should your story be illustrated with black-and-white pictures or color pictures? Why?

★ How might you organize the information you learned today? Explain.

October 26

● Is your story part of a series? Should it be? Explain.

★ Think about the topic of your reading. Would you rather read about it in a fiction book or a nonfiction book? Why?

October 27

● If you could change one part of the story, which part would you change?

★ Can you believe...

Daily Reading Prompts • ©The Mailbox® Books • TEC61269

Biography prompts on pages 100–103

October 28

● Write about one part of the story that made you smile.

★ If you were going to write about this topic, what information would you start with?

October 29

● Would you trust the main character to take care of your favorite pet? Why or why not?

★ Look at the table of contents. What would you like to learn about next?

October 30

● Think about the setting. Describe the loudest sound you might hear.

★ What did the author need to know before he or she started writing this text? Why?

October 31

● Imagine that you are at a Halloween party with the story's characters. What kind of costumes are the characters wearing? Why did they choose these costumes?

★ What do you still want to know about the topic?

Biography prompts on pages 100–103

November 1

● Today is National Authors' Day. Write a thank-you note to the author of your story. Tell him or her what you like about the story.

★ What do you already know about this topic? Explain.

Thank You

November 2

● Describe the story's problem. Tell how it might be solved.

★ What questions did you have that were answered today?

November 3

● Could your story take place in the fall? Why or why not?

★ Were you looking forward to reading the text today? Why or why not?

November 4

● Do you believe the narrator of this story is always truthful?

★ The best fact I learned from the author is…

Biography prompts on pages 100–103

November 5

● How does the story make you feel? Explain.

★ Does the author give facts and opinions about the topic? Explain.

November 6

● Which characters are the most interesting? Why?

★ How could you use the new information you learned today?

November 7

● How much time has passed since the beginning of the story? How do you know?

★ Should the author have written this text in a different way?

Biography prompts on pages 100–103

NOVEMBER

November 8

● Imagine you are a character who is not the main character. Write a summary of the story from your point of view.

★ Would you tell your teacher to read this text? Why or why not?

November 9

● Today is Guinness World Records Day. If the main character wanted to set a record, what kind would he or she set?

★ How do you know that this text is nonfiction instead of fiction?

November 10

● List the words that make it easy for you to imagine the story's setting. How do they help you?

★ Write one fact from your reading that you would share with a friend. Why did you choose this fact?

November 11

● What might happen next in the story? Why?

★ How does the author describe the topic you are reading about? How would you describe the topic?

Daily Reading Prompts • ©The Mailbox® Books • TEC61269

Biography prompts on pages 100–103

November 12

● What advice do you have for the main character?

★ Does the topic grab your interest? Why or why not?

November 13

● Could the order of events be changed without changing the outcome? Explain.

★ List some of the key vocabulary words from the text. Explain why each word is important to this text.

November 14

● What do you think the author is trying to say? Explain.

★ How could the people who publish the text make it easier to read? Explain.

November 15

● Look at the story again. Which picture is your favorite? Why?

★ I hope the author will talk about…

Biography prompts on pages 100–103

NOVEMBER

November 16

● What other stories does this one remind you of? How?

★ Choose a friend who would enjoy reading books by this author. Write a letter to your friend. Describe the text and the author.

November 17

● Imagine you are the main character. Write an entry in your journal. Describe your friends and family.

★ How do you think the author learned about the topic? Explain.

November 18

● Which event from the story is your least favorite? Why?

★ Would you change the way this text is organized? Explain.

November 19

● Pretend you are writing a newspaper article about the events in the story. What would the headline be? Why?

★ You would never guess that…

Daily Reading Prompts • ©The Mailbox® Books • TEC61269

Biography prompts on pages 100–103

November 20

● If this were a library book, would you check it out again? Why or why not?

★ If the author were in your classroom, what questions would you ask him or her? Which question would be the most important one? Explain.

November 21

● What is the most important message in your story? Explain.

★ What topic do you want to read about next? Why?

November 22

● Do you wish the author had chosen a different main character? Why or why not?

★ Which three things from the text will you share with your family?

Biography prompts on pages 100–103

November 23

● Imagine you are one of the characters. Write a journal entry about the story's problem.

★ I wonder whether the author will…

November 24

● Which part of this story do you think the author enjoyed writing the most? Explain your choice.

★ Did you know some of the facts in this text before you started reading? Explain.

November 25

● A friend asks you to name a story that is a lot like this one. What story do you name? Why?

★ What other topics do you think this author should write about? Why?

November 26

● What questions do you have about the setting? Explain.

★ Write one thing you read today that you knew before you started reading. Explain how you knew.

Daily Reading Prompts • ©The Mailbox® Books • TEC61269

Biography prompts on pages 100–103

November 27

● Is there an event in the story that could happen to you? Why or why not?

★ Could you write a fiction story about this topic? Why or why not?

November 28

● How do you think the story will end? Explain.

★ What types of pictures are in the text? For instance, are there photographs or drawings? Why do you think the author chose this type?

November 29

● Think about the last story you read. How are the characters in this story like the characters in that story?

★ Do you think the author left out any information about the topic? Explain.

November 30

● Imagine the author has asked you to write a sequel to the story. What will the title be? Why?

★ Do you think other people should read this text? Why or why not?

Biography prompts on pages 100–103

December 1

- ● What kind of award would you give the main character? Why?

- ★ Do you like the way this author writes? Why or why not?

December 2

- ● What is the story's theme? How does the theme fit into your life?

- ★ How do you find the meaning of a new word when you read it in the text?

December 3

- ● Why are you reading this story? Would you read it again? Why or why not?

- ★ Does the text have a table of contents? Does it need one? Why or why not?

December 4

Facts I Knew Before I Started Reading	Facts I've Learned Since I Started Reading

- ● If a character in your story wore a watch, what time would the watch show? How do you know?

- ★ Make a T chart with columns labeled "Facts I Knew Before I Started Reading" and "Facts I've Learned Since I Started Reading." Complete the chart.

Biography prompts on pages 100–103

December 5

● I predict…

★ Write a main idea from your text. Write three or more details that support the main idea.

December 6

● Choose one character from this story and one character from a different story. Explain why they would or would not be friends.

★ Does this book have an index? Why do you think the author made this choice about an index?

December 7

● Would you prefer to read this story by yourself or have someone read it to you? Why?

★ If you were putting this book in a bookstore, which section would you put it in? For instance, a book called *Sharks* might go with the animal books.

December 8

● Would you tell an older child to read this story? Why or why not?

★ Imagine your teacher asks you to make a vocabulary list for this text. Which words will you choose? Why?

Vocabulary List

Biography prompts on pages 100–103

Daily Reading Prompts • ©The Mailbox® Books • TEC61269

December 9

● Pretend you meet the main character. The character asks for your advice about the story's problem. What will you say?

★ The next text I read will be about... I know because...

December 10

● Write two or more words that were new to you before you started reading. Explain how you used the story to find out what the words meant.

★ Does the author think this is an important topic? How do you know?

December 11

● Think of a story event. How does this event remind you of something that is happening in the world?

★ Use five or more adjectives to describe the topic. Why did you choose these adjectives?

December 12

● Copy and complete one of these prompts:

I wish I had been one of the characters in the story because...

I am glad I was not one of the characters in the story because...

★ Write three key words from the text. Think of another text you have read that has a different topic. Would it have the same key words? Why or why not?

Daily Reading Prompts • ©The Mailbox® Books • TEC61269

Biography prompts on pages 100–103

December 13

● Who is telling the story? Could someone else tell it? Why or why not?

★ How is the topic of this text different from the topic of the last text you read?

December 14

● Why do you think the author chose this setting? Would you have chosen the same one? Why or why not?

★ Today's text was mainly about…

December 15

● Which parts of this story do you think could really happen? Explain.

★ Why are you reading this text?

December 16

● Do you think the main character is friendly? Why or why not?

★ Do you think the author added too many facts to this text? Why or why not?

Biography prompts on pages 100–103

December 17

● Which part of the story is your favorite so far? Why?

★ Today is Wright Brothers Day. On this day in 1903, the first powered flight took place. It is an important day in history. What historic day do you think the author of your text should write about? Why?

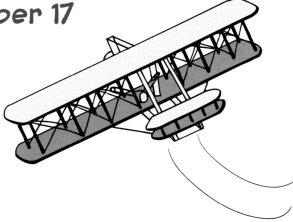

December 18

● Write two or more things you know about the plot that the main character does not. Explain.

★ A younger child asks you what this text is about. What will you say?

December 19

Jack and the Beanstalk

● Pretend that the author plans to rewrite the story. What would you ask him or her to change? Why?

★ Would you use your own money to buy this book? Why or why not?

December 20

● Which of the characters do you think you will remember the most? Explain.

★ Copy one sentence from the text that you think is very well written. Explain what you like about it.

Daily Reading Prompts • ©The Mailbox® Books • TEC61269

Biography prompts on pages 100–103

December 21

● How does reading this book make you feel? Why?

★ What information is the least interesting to you? Why?

December 22

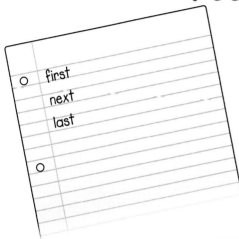

● Do you think the main character would rather be alone or with a group of friends? Why?

★ Write words from the text that show order. Explain how they help you understand what you're reading.

December 23

● Describe the story's problem from one character's point of view. Then describe it from a different character's point of view. Compare and contrast the descriptions.

★ Look at one of the pictures. Explain how it helps you understand what you read.

December 24

● Draw a symbol that stands for the main character. Explain your drawing.

★ The author includes key words about the topic. Do these words make it harder for you to read the text? Explain.

Biography prompts on pages 100–103

December 25

● Today is Christmas Day. You are making a Christmas feast. Which characters will you invite? Why?

★ Write three or more details you have learned about the topic. Explain each detail.

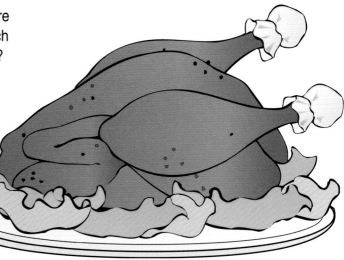

December 26

Read this!

● Choose a story event that you can picture in your head. List the words that help you picture the event.

★ Write an ad about this text. Use your ad to tell others why they should read this text.

December 27

● Why do you think the author chose this point of view?

★ How is the text organized? Are there chapters or subtitles? Does the organization make it easier for you to understand what you are reading? Why?

Biography prompts on pages 100–103

December 28

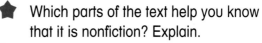

● Pretend you are a news reporter who is doing a story about the author. What will you ask him or her?

★ Which parts of the text help you know that it is nonfiction? Explain.

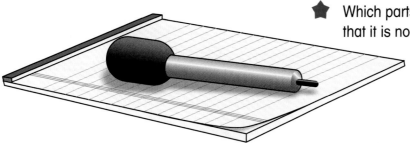

December 29

● Which character would you like to have as a classmate? Why?

★ Write two ideas from the text. Tell two or more ways these ideas are the same. Then tell two or more ways these ideas are different.

December 30

● Choose an event from the story. Retell it from a different point of view. Explain how it's different from the story.

★ Before I read this text, I already knew…

December 31.

● Today is New Year's Eve. It marks the end of the year. How would you change the end of the story? Why?

★ Today I read about… The text made me think…

The End

Biography prompts on pages 100–103

DECEMBER

January 1

● Pretend that you are one of the characters. Write a letter to another character. Tell him or her how you feel about the story.

★ When I read tomorrow, I hope the author will explain more about…

January 2

● Are you rushing to finish this story? Why or why not?

★ Write a fact that you are having trouble believing. Explain.

January 3

● What if the author had asked you to help him or her write the story? Which part would you want to write? Why?

★ Does this text have subheadings? If it does, do they help you understand what you're reading? If it does not, what subheadings would you add?

January 4

● Could this story have a winter setting? How do you know?

★ What else could you read that would help you understand this topic?

Daily Reading Prompts • ©The Mailbox® Books • TEC61269

Biography prompts on pages 100–103

January 5

● What famous person does the main character remind you of? Why?

★ Were you excited to start reading today? Why or why not?

January 6

● What do you think the main character worries about? How do you know?

★ The most important sentence I read today was... This is because...

January 7

● Does the author use words that affect your senses? Explain.

★ What did you read today that will help you in your classroom? Tell how it will help you.

January 8

● Rate the author's writing style. Use a scale of one star (dull) to five stars (thrilling). Tell why you chose this rating.

★ Think about the topic and the text you read today. Write five statements about the topic that are not true.

Biography prompts on pages 100–103

JANUARY

January 9

● How are you and the main character alike? How are you and the main character different?

★ Now I know…

January 10

● Plan a television show that could be made from this text. Describe the setting. Choose the actors who will be in the show.

★ Is there something about the topic that puzzles you? Explain.

January 11

● What does the author do to make you want to keep reading the story? Explain.

★ I already knew _____ about this topic. This makes me think the author…

January 12

● How would the story change if it took place somewhere else?

★ How did the clues in the text help you understand the words that you did not know?

Daily Reading Prompts • ©The Mailbox® Books • TEC61269

Biography prompts on pages 100–103

January 13

● What do you think the main character does in his or her free time? What makes you think that?

★ After reading this text, what do you want to learn more about?

January 14

● If you could choose a story to read, would you choose this one? Why or why not?

★ Think about another text you have read about this topic. Did that author agree with this author? Explain.

January 15

● What is the theme of this story? What other stories have you read that have the same theme?

★ Martin Luther King Jr. was born on this day in 1929. Dr. King wanted to make the world a better place. How could you use the information you've learned from this reading to make the world a better place?

January 16

● Which character do you enjoy reading about the most? Why?

★ Write three questions about your topic. Start each question with *Why*. Answer the questions.

Biography prompts on pages 100–103

JANUARY

JANUARY

January 17

● How does the setting of this story remind you of a place you have been?

★ I wonder, will this reading be about…?

January 18

● Which character has changed the most? Explain.

★ What does the author do to make this topic more interesting?

January 19

● The next time I see this author's name, I will think…

★ Which facts from the text would an older person want to know? Why?

January 20

● If you were the main character, what would you do next?

★ Write two facts from the text. Use information from the text to prove the facts.

Biography prompts on pages 100–103

January 21

● What is the most important part of the story? Why?

★ My favorite fact from the text is _____ because…

January 22

● Would it be easier for you to understand the text if someone read it to you? Why or why not?

★ Does this text have a glossary? Does it need one? Why or why not?

January 23

● Think about the setting. Describe the sounds you would hear there.

★ How has reading this text changed your opinion about the topic?

Biography prompts on pages 100–103

January 24

● I wish the author had…

★ What words does the author use that let you know that this text is nonfiction?

January 25

● Which of the characters would you ask for help if you were in trouble? Why?

★ After reading this text, I will know…

HELP!

January 26

red, pretty, soft

● Choose one person, place, or thing the author describes. Write your own description.

★ Does the text include facts and opinions about the topic? Explain your answer with examples from your reading.

January 27

● What did you learn from the story? How can you use what you've learned from the story?

★ What do you think the author thought about before he chose this topic?

Biography prompts on pages 100–103

January 28

● Write about an important event from the story. Explain why it happened.

★ List five or more topics you think this author could write about. Tell why you think so.

January 29

● Write a letter to the author. Tell him or her what you think of the story. Use details to explain how you feel.

★ Pretend that you wrote the text you read today. Write in your journal. Tell how you feel about the work you have done on the text.

January 30

● How does the problem in the story remind you of a problem you've read about in another story? Compare the way the problems were solved.

★ List three or more words that you think the author should not have used. Tell which words he or she should have used instead. Explain.

city
~~metropolis~~

January 31

● Think about authors of other books you have read. Which one of them could have written a story like the one you're reading now? Explain.

★ The author has arranged the information by…

Biography prompts on pages 100–103

February 1

● How do you think the main character feels about the other characters? Explain.

⭐ Pretend you are a news reporter who is doing a story on this topic. Choose three key points from the text. Write your story.

February 2

● Today is Groundhog Day. If the groundhog sees his shadow today, winter will last for six more weeks. What season is your story set in? How do you know?

⭐ Draw a Venn diagram. Use it to compare the facts in this text to the facts you already knew about this topic.

February 3

● How does the story end? How would you change the ending if you could? Why?

⭐ If you finish this text today, what would you like to read tomorrow?

February 4

● Describe the way the story makes you feel. Tell why it makes you feel this way.

⭐ What did the author think you already knew about the topic before you started reading? How do you know?

FEBRUARY

Biography prompts on pages 100–103

February 5

- How does the author involve you in the story?

- Today I found out...

February 6

- Does the main character show determination? How do you know?

- What changes would you make to the author's writing?

February 7

- As I was reading today, I remembered...

- Would you like to have lunch with the author? Why or why not?

FEBRUARY

FICTION

NONFICTION

F E B R U A R Y

February 8

● Choose a part of the story that you think the author had to plan a lot before it was written. Tell why you think so.

★ Do you think the author enjoyed writing this text? Why or why not?

February 9

● Are there any characters that could have been left out of the story? Explain.

★ If something is current, it is up-to-date. Do you think the information in this text is current? Why or why not?

February 10

● Do you think this story's events are in the right order? Why or why not?

★ What if the author hadn't written about this topic? Do you think someone else would have? Why or why not?

February 11

● Is the main character like kids your age? Why or why not?

★ What ideas did the author leave out of this text? Explain.

Daily Reading Prompts • ©The Mailbox® Books • TEC61269

Biography prompts on pages 100–103

February 12

- Does the story make you laugh or cry? Why or why not?

- Today I read… That makes me think that part of the text will be about…

February 13

- Why do you think the author chose to tell the story from this point of view?

- When I write on my own, I am going to remember the way this author…

February 14

- Today is Valentine's Day. Make a valentine card for one of the characters. Tell the character why you like reading about him or her.

- How many times have you used a dictionary while reading this text? How many more times do you think you will need to use a dictionary before you finish reading? Explain.

HAPPY VALENTINE'S DAY

Biography prompts on pages 100–103

February 15

- Do you want to read other books about the main character? Why or why not?

- Pretend you are using this text to teach a younger child about this topic. Write a summary of what you will say to the child.

February 16

- Think about the story's theme. Pretend your teacher has asked you to write a story that has a theme like this one. Make a plan.

- Write one important fact from the text. Tell why it is important.

February 17

- If you went on a trip to the story's setting, what would you pack?

- Describe your favorite picture in the text. How does it help you understand what you are reading?

February 18

- If you were one of the characters, how would you have solved the problem? Why?

- This part of the book made me think of a time at home when…

Biography prompts on pages 100–103

February 19

- When does this story take place? How do you know?

- ⭐ I think the author is trying to say…

February 20

- Do you think the author knows some kids your age? Why or why not?

- ⭐ When I read…, it made me wonder about…

February 21

- The turning point is the part of the story when the main character has to make an important choice. What is the turning point of this story? Would you have made the same choice? Why or why not?

- ⭐ This book reminds me of something my teacher told me because…

February 22

- George Washington was born on this day in 1732. If the main character were going to be the president of a club, what kind of club would it be?

- ⭐ What can you do to learn whether or not what the author has written is true?

Biography prompts on pages 100–103

FEBRUARY

February 23

● Draw an interesting event from the story. Draw yourself and a speech bubble in the picture. In the speech bubble, write what you will say to the characters.

★ What are you still hoping to learn about this topic?

February 24

● What do you think the main character's goal is? How do you know?

★ Do you think the author would make a good teacher? Why or why not?

February 25

glee
joy
pleasant

● Good authors use words to set the mood of the story. What words does this author use? What do the words tell you about the story?

★ Why should other people read this text? Explain.

February 26

● Pretend the author has asked you to write a chapter to add to the book. Write a summary of the chapter you will add.

★ Your teacher has time to read only one page of this text. Which page will you ask him or her to read? Why?

Biography prompts on pages 100–103

February 27

● If I could rewrite one event from the story, I would choose…

☆ Choose two ideas from your reading. Write two ways they are different and two ways they are alike.

February 28

● Is the main character brave? How do you know?

☆ An editor checks the facts in the text before it is printed. Imagine you are the editor. Choose three facts you will check. Explain your choices.

February 29

● Every four years, the calendar has 366 days instead of 365. The extra day is February 29, and it's called Leap Day. What if the characters had an extra day to solve the problem? What would happen? Why?

☆ Choose one picture from the text. Write a new caption for the picture. Use key words from the text in your caption.

Biography prompts on pages 100–103

Daily Reading Prompts • ©The Mailbox® Books • TEC61269

March 1

● Is this a mystery story? How do you know?

★ What is the copyright date of the text? Do you think the facts have changed since the text was published? Why or why not?

March 2

● Today is Dr. Seuss's birthday. Dr. Seuss used rhyming words and fun pictures to make his books appeal to kids. What does the author of this story do to make it appeal to kids?

★ To be curious means to wonder about something. Does this text make you curious about the topic? Why or why not?

March 3

● I would like to meet the main character because…

★ Write one question that can be answered by reading the text. Then write one question that asks for the reader's opinion about the topic. Answer the questions.

March 4

● Did one of the characters make a mistake? If so, how did the mistake hurt the other characters? How did the character fix the mistake?

★ Before you start reading, draw a large speech bubble on a sheet of paper. As you're reading, write your questions in the speech bubble. Find the answer to each question.

Daily Reading Prompts • ©The Mailbox® Books • TEC61269

Biography prompts on pages 100–103

March 5

● How does the problem start? Explain.

★ Make a web about the topic. Put a main idea in the center and draw a circle around it. Then write three or more supporting details around the main idea. Draw a circle around each one. Connect the detail circles to the main idea circle.

March 6

● What is the author trying to teach you? Explain.

★ Write three or more things from your life that you can relate to this topic. Explain.

March 7

● Do you think the story could really happen? Why or why not?

★ What do you think the author's goal is? How do you know?

March 8

● One part of the story that is not interesting is…

I feel this way because…

★ What do you think the author did to research this topic before he or she started writing? Explain.

Biography prompts on pages 100–103

MARCH

March 9

● Who is the hero in the story? What makes the character a hero?

★ The last text I read was…

This text is the same as that text because…

This text is different from that text because…

March 10

● On this day in 1876, Alexander Graham Bell made the first telephone call. If you could call the main character, what would you say to him or her?

★ I wonder why the author…

March 11

● List the names of three or more characters. Write a short description of each one.

★ Are there other facts you would like to add to the text? Explain.

March 12

● Choose one quote that tells a lot about the main character. Copy it on your paper. Explain your choice.

★ Do you think the vocabulary in this text is too easy, just right, or too hard? Explain.

Daily Reading Prompts • ©The Mailbox® Books • TEC61269

Biography prompts on pages 100–103

March 13

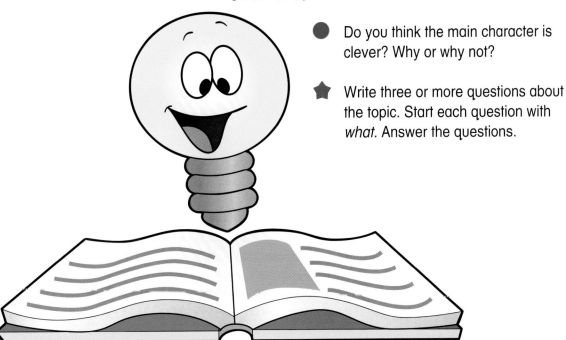

● Do you think the main character is clever? Why or why not?

★ Write three or more questions about the topic. Start each question with *what*. Answer the questions.

March 14

● Today is International Ask a Question Day. If the author could ask you questions about the story, what do you think he or she would ask? Why?

★ If you find another text written by this author, will you read it? Why or why not?

March 15

● Are you glad you read this story? Why or why not?

★ The thing I like best about this text is…

Biography prompts on pages 100–103

March 16

● How does the setting change from the beginning of the story to the end? Explain.

★ Do you think this author knows how to write for kids your age? Why or why not?

March 17

● Pretend you are the main character. Do you like the way the author is telling your story? Why or why not?

★ Sometimes an author's writing style makes you feel as though he or she is talking right to you. Do you feel this way as you read this text? Why or why not?

March 18

● Choose a character from another story who might like to be friends with the main character in this story. Explain your choice.

★ Would a scientist want to read this text? Why or why not?

March 19

● This story's point of view is important because…

★ How could you use this text to help you write a fictional story?

Daily Reading Prompts • ©The Mailbox® Books • TEC61269

Biography prompts on pages 100–103

March 20

● What does the main character learn about himself or herself in the story? Explain.

★ I would like to ask the author why he or she used the words… because I think…

March 21

● Would your best friend enjoy this story? Why or why not?

★ For which part of the text do you think the author had the hardest time finding the information? Explain.

March 22

● What is the theme of this story? Why do you think the author chose this theme?

★ How will reading this text help you with your school work?

March 23

● Did an event in the story make you feel angry or sad? Why or why not?

★ I could hardly believe it when I read…

Biography prompts on pages 100–103

March 24

● Is the main character different at the end of the story? If so, how?

★ As I look at the pictures, I really wonder…

March 25

● The setting of the story includes the time period. A story may take place in the past, present, or future. If this story were in a different time period, how would it change?

★ Write the name of another nonfiction text. Tell two or more ways that text is like this text. Then tell two or more ways that text is not like this text.

March 26

● The plot includes the beginning, middle, and end of the story. Draw three squares on your paper. Label them *beginning, middle,* and *end.* In each square, write matching events from the story.

★ Because I have read this text, the next thing I would like to read is…

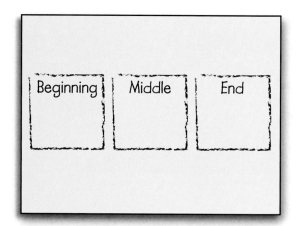

| Beginning | Middle | End |

March 27

● If you were having a party, would you invite the main character? Why or why not?

★ One star stands for the easiest text you have ever read. Five stars stands for the hardest text you have ever read. How many stars would you give this text? Why?

Biography prompts on pages 100–103

March 28

● Would you tell a younger child to read this story? Why or why not?

★ Does this text have subheadings? If so, what other subheadings would you add? If not, what subheadings would you write for this text?

March 29

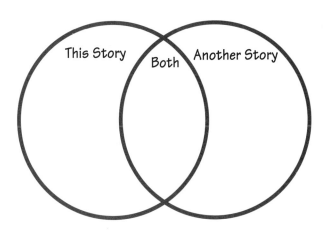

This Story   Both   Another Story

● Draw a Venn diagram. Compare the setting in this story to the setting in another story you have read.

★ Would you give this author an award for great writing? Why or why not?

March 30

● What is the theme of this story? Do you think a lot of kids will understand this theme? Why or why not?

★ The author is going to write another book about this topic. What facts should he or she use in the next text? Explain.

March 31

● What made you want to read this story? Explain.

★ List some cause-and-effect examples from this text.

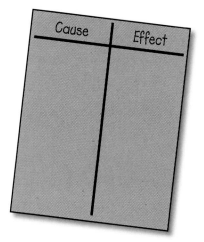

Cause	Effect

Biography prompts on pages 100–103

APRIL

April 1

● Today is April Fools' Day, a day when people play jokes on each other. Which character in the story would be good at playing jokes? Why?

★ Reread one page of the text. Write a summary of the page.

April 2

● Is there an event in the story that could never happen to you? Explain.

★ Write three or more true statements about the topic. Then write three or more false statements about the topic.

April 3

● Does the title match the story? Why or why not?

★ What does the author do to help you understand the new words he or she uses? Explain.

April 4

● Could this story take place in the spring? Why or why not?

★ Talk with a friend about the text you're reading. Does your friend agree with the author's point of view? Why or why not?

Biography prompts on pages 100–103

April 5

● Which characters remind you of real people? Why?

★ Think about the way the author uses words. Would you want to read another book by this author? Use examples from the text to explain why or why not.

April 6

● Doing the right thing is a common theme. Do you think the main character does the right thing?

★ Think about what you have read. Why should you share this information with others?

April 7

● Choose two characters from the story. Use a Venn diagram to compare them.

★ This is my opinion of the facts I read today…

April 8

● How would you tell an artist to draw the setting of the story?

★ April is National Kite Month. People all over the country celebrate kites with events like fairs and kite-making classes. What kind of events could you have to honor your topic?

Biography prompts on pages 100–103

APRIL

April 9

● If the main character were famous, what would he or she be famous for?

★ Your teacher is looking for an expert on this topic. Will you raise your hand? Why or why not?

April 10

● This is a great story because…

★ What descriptive words does the author use? How do they help you understand what you're reading?

April 11

● Which event in the text surprised you so much that you're not sure it's possible? Why?

★ If this text were a newspaper story, what would the headline be? Why?

Daily Reading Prompts • ©The Mailbox® Books • TEC61269

Biography prompts on pages 100–103

April 12

● What is the story's theme? How does it make you feel? Do you think the author wants you to feel this way? Why or why not?

★ The most important thing you need to know about this topic is... Why?

April 13

● If I could be any character in the story, I would be...

★ The author could make this book even more interesting by...

April 14

● Which event is the most important one you read about today? How do you think it will change the outcome? Why?

★ How would you describe this author's writing style? Why?

April 15

● Think about the setting. What sights would you see?

★ Make a timeline to show some of the information from this text.

Biography prompts on pages 100–103

APRIL

APRIL

April 16

● Think about the last story you read. What is one way that story is like this story?

★ The author does not expect readers to know...

April 17

● What kind of person do you think the author is? Why?

★ If a family member asks you what you read today, what will you say? Explain.

April 18

● The main character moves into your neighborhood. Will the two of you become friends? Why or why not?

★ Good nonfiction authors state facts clearly. Does this author do that? Explain.

April 19

● I felt happy when I read...

★ Which three details does the author think are the most important? What makes you think that?

Biography prompts on pages 100–103

April 20

- I think the main character wants to…

- Your teacher asks you to make a glossary for this text. Which words will you put in it? Why?

April 21

- Would you rather read this story by yourself or with a partner? Why?

- Write a summary of what you read today.

April 22

- Today is National Jelly Bean Day. Jelly beans are a favorite treat of many people. What kind of treats would the main character like? Why?

- What funny thing did this text remind you of? Why?

April 23

- What do you think the main character will be like in ten years? Why?

- If you make a list of the ten best things you have ever read, will this text be on the list? Explain.

APRIL

Biography prompts on pages 100–103

APRIL

April 24

● If you could rewrite the story, would you add more describing words? Why or why not?

★ What else have you read or heard about this topic? How did that help you as you read?

tasty
sweet
pretty

April 25

● Think about what you read today. Why did the main character do what he or she did? How do you know?

★ I think I know how the author feels about this topic because…

April 26

● The way the author writes reminds me of another story I have read because…

★ Before you started reading, what did you know about the topic? What did you not know about it?

April 27

● If you could add a character to the story, what kind of character would you add? Would the character change the plot? Why or why not?

★ Copy one sentence from the text that you have questions about. Explain what your questions are.

Daily Reading Prompts • ©The Mailbox® Books • TEC61269

Biography prompts on pages 100–103

April 28

● What does the main character value? How do you know?

★ I think the author did a good job of explaining…

April 29

facts | opinions

● How does the story begin? Would you begin this story the same way? Why or why not?

★ Make a T chart with the headings "Facts" and "Opinions." Complete the chart with statements from the text.

April 30

● What do you think you have learned about the author after reading the story? Why?

★ Write three questions about the text. Start each question with "What did I learn about…" Answer the questions.

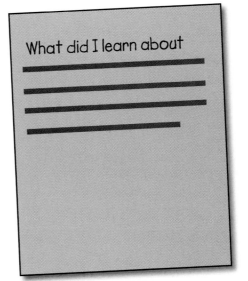

What did I learn about

Biography prompts on pages 100–103

May 1

● Which part of the story do you like the least? Why?

★ What has the author done to make this topic more interesting?

May 2

● Would you watch a movie that was made about this book? Why or why not?

★ Make predictions about the rest of the text. After you read, revise your predictions.

Popcorn SODA

May 3

● Make a list of people in your class who would enjoy reading this story. Explain why they would enjoy it.

★ Choose five words from today's reading that you will use in your own writing. Explain each choice.

May 4

There are many ways to eat healthily.

You can find many ways to eat healthy foods.

● If you had the same problem the main character has, what would you do? Why?

★ Copy one of the main ideas from the text. Rewrite the main idea in your own words. Then write details that support the main idea. Use the text to help you.

M A Y

Biography prompts on pages 100–103

May 5

● Do you want to keep reading the story? Why or why not?

★ Reread the first paragraph. How does it help you understand the rest of the text?

May 6

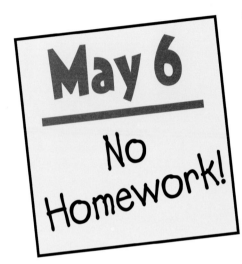

May 6

No Homework!

● Today is No Homework Day. Write a letter to your teacher. Tell him or her why you want to read your story instead of doing homework tonight.

★ Write three sentences about the text you read today. Start each sentence with "I learned…"

May 7

● What is the main character's greatest strength? Why?

★ Reread two sections of the text and compare them. How are they alike? How are they different?

Biography prompts on pages 100–103

May 8

● I was worried about the characters when I read…

★ Before I started reading, I didn't know that… Now, I know…

May 9

● Write a letter to a friend. Tell your friend what you like or don't like about this author's writing.

★ Does the author make it easy or hard for you to understand the facts? Explain.

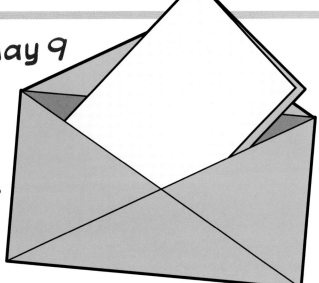

May 10

● If I could meet the author, I would tell him that he should have…

★ Copy three topic sentences from your text. How do you know these are topic sentences?

May 11

● What mistakes do you think the main character makes? What would you tell him or her to do differently?

★ Today is Eat What You Want Day. If this author wrote a book about your favorite food, would you read it? Why or why not?

Biography prompts on pages 100–103

May 12

● Pretend that the main character has won a dream vacation. Where will he or she go? Why?

★ Do you think there are too many, too few, or just enough facts in this text? Why?

May 13

● Which part of the story do you think the author had the hardest time writing? Why?

★ Rate this text. Use a scale of one star (Where are the pictures?) to five stars (Way too many pictures!). Explain your rating.

May 14

● Does this story take place in the future? How do you know?

★ How would you prove that the facts in this text are true? Explain.

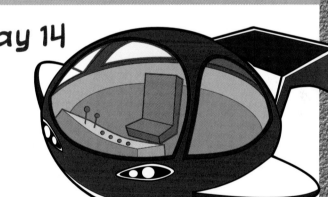

May 15

● Retitle the story. Explain your choice.

★ Good nonfiction is clear and easy to understand. Do you think this text is good nonfiction? Why or why not?

Biography prompts on pages 100–103

May 16

● Do you like the main character? Why or why not?

★ I wish I could find out more about…

May 17

● If the story took place in a different time period, how would it change?

★ After reading this text, do you want to learn more about this topic? Why or why not?

May 18

● A magic genie grants the main character three wishes. What will he or she wish for?

★ Write three facts about this topic. Then rate the facts from one star (least important) to three stars (most important).

May 19

● Write three words that describe the way the story makes you feel. Explain your choices.

★ List four key words from the text. In what other texts might you find these key words?

Biography prompts on pages 100–103

May 20

● Is this story an adventure? Why or why not?

★ Today's reading made me really curious about…

May 21

● What kind of birthday present would you give the main character? Why?

★ Think about the facts you read today. Make a chart to show where in the text the facts are found.

May 22

● Think about the events of the story. Could you change their order without changing the outcome? Why or why not?

★ What did you read today that you will tell your friends about? Explain.

May 23

● What questions do you have about the end of the story? Explain.

★ An older child wants to know whether she should read this text. What will you tell her?

Biography prompts on pages 100–103

FICTION ●

NONFICTION ★

May 24

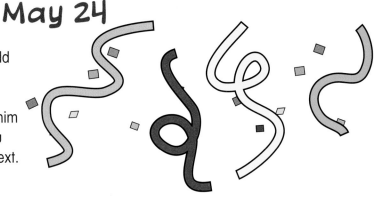

● Which one of the characters would you invite to a party? Why?

★ Write a letter to the author. Tell him or her how you will use what you have learned from reading this text.

May 25

● Which character is telling the story? How do you know?

★ Before you started reading, did you think you would like this text? Why or why not?

May 26

● The main character travels to your home. Will he or she like visiting there? Why or why not?

★ Choose a paragraph and read the first sentence. Is it the topic sentence? Why or why not?

May 27

● The author holds my attention by…

★ What helpful things did you learn today? Explain.

Daily Reading Prompts • ©The Mailbox® Books • TEC61269

Biography prompts on pages 100–103

May 28

● Write a different ending for the story. How will the rest of the story change to fit your new ending?

★ Make a list of the things you knew about this topic before you started reading. Did knowing these things help you understand the text? Why or why not?

May 29

● Which part of the story is the most exciting? Why?

★ What questions do you still have about the topic? If you can't find the answers in the text, where will you look to find them?

May 30

● What would your life be like if you were one of the characters in the story?

★ Write one fact from the text that you know is true. How do you know it's true?

May 31

● Does the main character remind you of someone you know? Explain.

★ What can you learn from the pictures in your text? Are there other pictures that should be in the text?

Biography prompts on pages 100–103

JUNE

June 1

● Today is Pen Pal Day. Which character would you want as your pen pal? Why?

★ Which fact from the text do you think is the least interesting? Which is the most interesting? Why?

Pen Pal

Pen Pal

June 2

● I wish the author had…

★ Because I read _____, I think…

June 3

● Where and when does this story take place? How do you know?

★ How did you feel about this topic before you started reading? How has your opinion changed?

June 4

● How does this story remind you of another story you have read or heard? Explain.

★ Did the author give you enough facts to help you understand the topic? Explain.

Biography prompts on pages 100–103

June 5

● Would you want to read this story again? Why or why not?

★ What do you like about the way this text is written? Why?

June 6

● Do the characters know how to cooperate? How do you know?

★ Which fact will you remember the most from what you read today? Why?

June 7

● What might happen to the characters after the story's end? Write to explain what happens to each one.

★ When I see this author's name on another text, I will think…

Biography prompts on pages 100–103

JUNE

June 8

● How would you describe the main character to your friend?

★ The author has asked you to draw a picture to add to the text. What will you draw? Why?

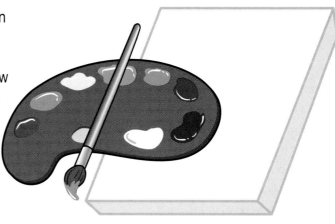

June 9

● Are you curious about the end of the story? Why or why not?

★ What key words helped you understand this text? How did you learn the meanings of these words?

June 10

● What is something the main character says that reminds you of something you would say? Why?

★ Does this text need to be read in order from start to finish? Why or why not?

June 11

● How long do you think it took the author to write this story? Explain.

★ Write five true statements about this topic. Use the text to help you.

Biography prompts on pages 100–103

June 12

- The author made me laugh when...

- ⭐ Are you eager to finish reading this text? Why or why not?

June 13

- Think about a time when you had a problem like the one in the story. What did you do?

- ⭐ I would like to meet the author because...

June 14

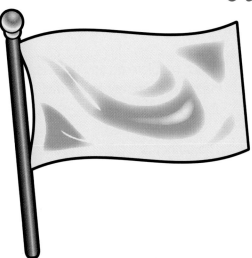

- Today is Flag Day. Each part of the American flag is an important symbol. If you were asked to design a flag for this book, what kind of symbols would you use? What would each symbol mean?

- ⭐ Write one fact from the text that you think is not as important as the other facts. Explain your choice.

June 15

- What mistakes do you think the main character makes? Explain.

- ⭐ Which parts of this text would you share with a younger child? Why?

Biography prompts on pages 100–103

June 16

● Is the main character honest? How do you know?

★ Choose one item that is described in the text. Draw a picture of it. Write a caption for your picture.

June 17

● The setting is important because...

★ Do the facts in this text match what you already know about the topic? Why or why not?

June 18

● Which problem do you think is the most important to the main character? Why?

★ The author is a guest on your favorite talk show. What do you hope the host asks him or her? Why?

Daily Reading Prompts • ©The Mailbox® Books • TEC61269

Biography prompts on pages 100–103

June 19

● Do you think the main character will learn a lesson? Explain.

★ Because I read this text, I know how to…

June 20

● Why do you think the author chose this setting? Do you think the story would be as good if the author had chosen another setting? Why or why not?

★ List two main ideas from your reading today. Tell two or more ways they are alike. Then tell two or more ways they are different.

June 21

● Do you think the author has spent much time around children? Why or why not?

★ I wish I could tell the author…

June 22

● Has it been easy for you to predict the next event? Why or why not?

★ The most important thing I have learned about this author is _____ because…

Biography prompts on pages 100–103

June 23

● What is the story's lesson? How can you use what you've learned to help a friend? Explain.

★ Find one sentence in the text that makes you curious. Copy it on your paper. Explain your choice.

June 24

● Are you more like or unlike the main character? Why?

★ Rate this text and explain your rating. Use this scale:

★ = too many new vocabulary words (This text is hard to understand.)

★ ★ = just enough new vocabulary words (This text is interesting.)

★ ★ ★ = not enough new vocabulary words (I would learn more if there were more words that are new to me.)

June 25

● How does the story make you feel? Why does it make you feel this way?

★ What did the author do to make this text fun to read? Explain.

June 26

● Have you visited a setting that was the same as this setting? Explain.

★ What kind of map would you add to this text? Why?

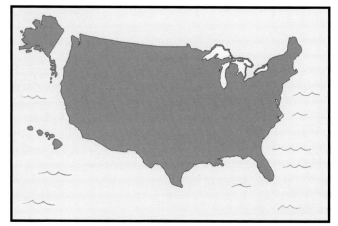

JUNE

Daily Reading Prompts • ©The Mailbox® Books • TEC61269

Biography prompts on pages 100–103

June 27

● "Happy Birthday to You" was composed on June 27, 1859. Would you give this book to your friend as a birthday gift? Why or why not?

★ Choose two facts that you still have questions about. Write a letter to the author. Ask him or her to explain the two facts.

June 28

● Why do you think the author chose this title? Explain.

★ Pretend your teacher asks you to teach a lesson about this topic. What three main ideas will you tell your classmates? Why?

June 29

● Would you have told the story in the same order? Why or why not?

★ Why are you reading this text? Would you read it again? Why or why not?

June 30

● How do you know what the characters are thinking or feeling? Explain.

★ If you were the author, would you be proud of this text? Why or why not?

Biography prompts on pages 100–103

Daily Reading Prompts • ©The Mailbox® Books • TEC61269

July 1

● Did you think you would like this story before you read it? Were you correct? Why or why not?

⭐ Today's text made me think about...

July 2

● Finish the sentence "This setting reminds me of..." Use details from the story as you write.

⭐ How do you think the author learned about this topic? Explain.

July 3

● If I were one of the characters, I would think...

⭐ How is this text different from the last text you read? Explain.

July 4

● When you see another story about this character, what will you do? Why?

⭐ Today is the Fourth of July. It is the nation's birthday. If this author wrote a text about the Fourth of July, would you read it? Why or why not?

Daily Reading Prompts • ©The Mailbox® Books • TEC61269

Biography prompts on pages 100–103

July 5

● Some words can bring back strong memories. Choose two or more words from the story and tell what memories they bring back for you. Explain your answer.

★ What did you learn from the text? Now that you know this, what changes will you make in your life? Why?

July 6

● Which character would you like to have for a next-door neighbor? Why?

★ Which fact from your reading was the most important? Why?

July 7

● Would you like to go to the author's house for dinner? Why or why not?

★ What questions do you still have? Where will you look to find the answers?

July 8

● What is the problem in this story? What is the solution? Do you think it is the best solution? Why or why not?

★ How can you tell that this text is nonfiction? Explain.

Biography prompts on pages 100–103

FICTION

NONFICTION

JULY

July 9

● I wonder if the main character will…

⭐ Which part of this text do you think was the easiest for the author to write? Why?

July 10

● If the main character were going to read a story, would he or she like this one? Why or why not?

⭐ Some of these facts may not be true because…

July 11

● Who is telling the story? If you could talk with this person, what would you ask about the story? Why?

⭐ Write five or more sentences about what you've read today.

July 12

rounded
flat
salty
smooth
intelligent

● How did the story start? Did you like the beginning? Why or why not?

⭐ List five or more adjectives from the text. How do these words help you understand what you are reading?

94

Daily Reading Prompts • ©The Mailbox® Books • TEC61269

Biography prompts on pages 100–103

July 13

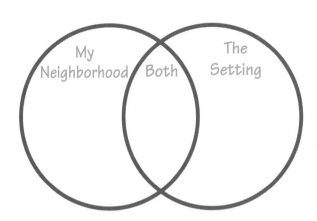

My Neighborhood Both The Setting

● Draw a Venn diagram. Use it to compare the setting of this story to your neighborhood.

⭐ I wonder why the author didn't…

July 14

● What does the author do to make this story exciting? Explain.

⭐ Which part of this text should the author be most proud of? Why?

July 15

● Would you read this story to the teacher you had last year? Why or why not?

⭐ Pretend the author is coming to meet your class. You will introduce him or her to the class. What will you say? Why?

July 16

● Which character changes the most? How does the character change?

⭐ Which fact from the text is the easiest to understand? Why?

Biography prompts on pages 100–103

July 17

● Which character is the hardest worker? How do you know?

⭐ Your teacher has asked you to make a dictionary for this text. Which words will you put in your dictionary? Why?

July 18

● How would the story change if the character were ten years older? Explain.

⭐ Make a T chart with two headings: "Facts I Understand" and "Facts I Don't Understand." Complete the chart with facts from the text.

Facts I Understand	Facts I Don't Understand

July 19

● How does this book remind you of a movie you have seen? Which movie does it remind you of? Why?

⭐ Could you use the facts from this text to do a job? Explain.

July 20

● On July 20, 1969, people landed on the moon for the first time. Would the main character be brave enough to fly to the moon? Why or why not?

⭐ How will you share this information with others? Explain.

Daily Reading Prompts • ©The Mailbox® Books • TEC61269

Biography prompts on pages 100–103

July 21

● What kind of award would you give the author? Why?

★ Rate the pictures in the text. Explain your rating. Use the scale shown.

★ = There are too many pictures. I'm confused!

★★ = There are just enough pictures. They help me understand the text.

★★★ = There are not enough pictures. I don't understand.

July 22

● I would tell the author I didn't like…because…

★ What one fact did you read that you think your teacher may not know? Explain.

July 23

● Do you think the main character will do the same thing the next time he or she faces a problem? Why or why not?

★ Does the author care about this topic? How do you know?

July 24

● Do the characters show kindness to each other? How do you know?

★ The thing that is most interesting about this topic is…

Biography prompts on pages 100–103

July 25

● Do any of the characters remind you of a person you know? Why or why not?

★ Do you think this author could write a fiction story? Explain.

U
L
Y

July 26

● What is the main character's greatest weakness? Why?

★ Your teacher asks you to list the best nonfiction texts you have read. Would this text be on the list? Why or why not?

July 27

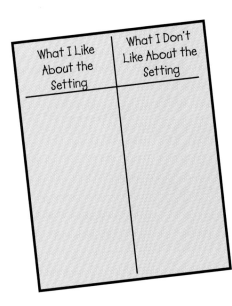

What I Like About the Setting	What I Don't Like About the Setting

● Make a T chart with two headings: "What I Like About the Setting" and "What I Don't Like About the Setting." Complete the chart with ideas from the story.

★ Write a new title for the text you read today. Explain your title.

98
Daily Reading Prompts • ©The Mailbox® Books • TEC61269

Biography prompts on pages 100–103

July 28

● Does this story take place in the past, present, or future? How do you know?

★ Some facts are interesting but not very important. Write two or more facts from the text that are interesting but not important.

July 29

● If there were a thunderstorm, would the main character be afraid? How do you know?

★ Make a timeline to explain the text. Use order words to help you.

July 30

● Do you think the author wants you to like all the characters? Why or why not?

★ Do you think the facts in this text will be current in ten years? Why or why not?

July 31

● How is this story different from other stories you have read? Explain.

★ Would this text make a good movie? Why or why not?

Biography prompts on pages 100–103

BIOGRAPHY

- Does this person's life remind you of anyone you know? Explain.

- One interesting thing I learned about this person is...

- If you could meet this person, what would you ask him or her? Why?

- Which fact about this person has surprised you the most? Why?

- Would you like to have lunch with this person? Why or why not?

- I think the person I read about today would like to read...

- I think my teacher would be surprised to learn that the person I am reading about...

- Pretend that you are the person you are reading about. Use your senses to describe the place where you live.

- What does the author do to make this text more interesting? Explain.

- How does this person show kindness to others? Explain.

- Is this person strong? Why or why not?

- Describe one problem this person had. What did the person do? Would you have done the same thing? Why or why not?

- Would you want to be friends with this person? Why or why not?

- Imagine that you are this person. Write a journal entry about your day.

- How do you think the author feels about this person? Why?

- How do you think the author learned about the person he or she wrote about? Explain.

- List five facts about this person. Circle the most important fact. Explain your choice.

- Make a timeline of the events you read about today.

- You are going to visit this person. What will you need to pack? Why?

- Name two things you like about this person. Explain.

- Is this person brave? How do you know?

- What did you know about this person before you started reading? How did this help you understand the text?

- Make a T chart with two headings: "Facts" and "Opinions." Complete the chart with ideas from the text.

- Think about the events in this person's life. What is the most important event you have read about so far? Why?

- Rate this text. Explain your rating. Use this scale:
  ★ = not interesting   ★★ = interesting   ★★★ = very interesting

- What questions do you still have about this person's life? How will you find the answers to these questions?

BIOGRAPHY

BIOGRAPHY

- Would you like to live next door to this person? Why or why not?

- Write a new title for this biography. Explain your title.

- Make a timeline of the person's life. Use the order words to help you.

- How does this person remind you of another famous person? Explain.

- What was the most important thing you learned about this person's life?

- The person I read about today is most known for...

- How will you describe this person to your best friend?

- Draw a Venn diagram. Use it to compare your life to this person's life.

- Is this person clever? How do you know?

- Name one good thing that happened to this person. Why did it happen?

- This biography reminds me of...

- Why did you want to read about this person?

- Would you like to spend a day with the person you read about? Why or why not?

- Do you think the author wants you to like this person? Why or why not?

- I wish the author had written more about this person's _____ because...

- What would you tell a younger child about this person? Why?

- Would you want to see a movie about this person's life? Why or why not?

- Who else should this author write about? Why?

- Who would you like this person to meet? Why?

- Why do you think this author chose to write about this person?

- What words does the author use to help you understand the setting? Explain.

- Describe one event in the person's life. Why do you think it happened the way it did?

- Your teacher asks you to give a speech about this person. What will you say?

- When was this text written? Do you think the facts about this person are still true? Why or why not?

BIOGRAPHY

_____

name

My Reading Journal

Daily Reading Prompts • ©The Mailbox® Books • TEC61269

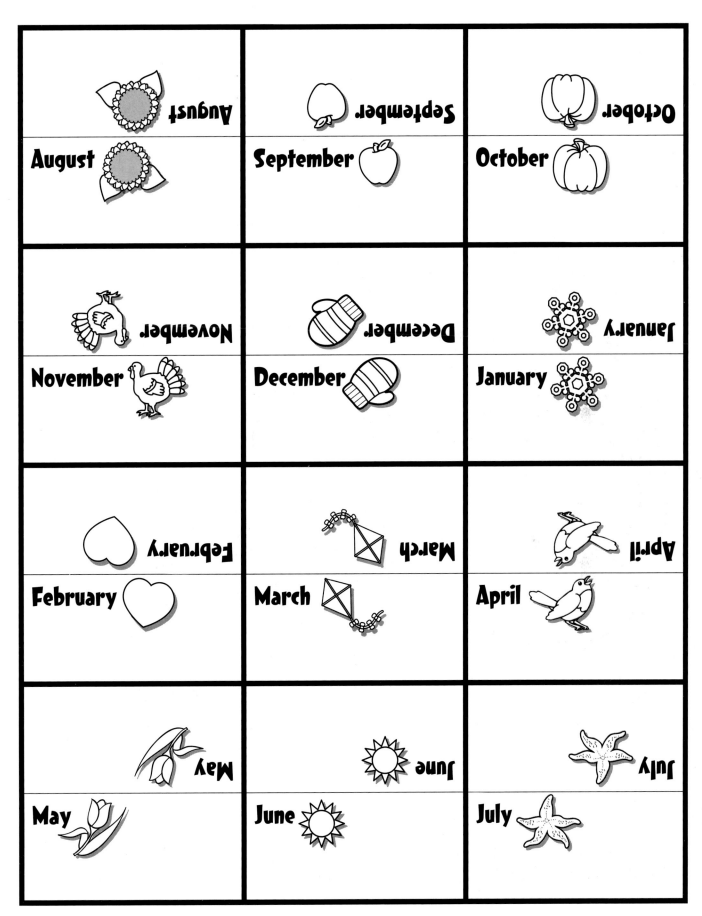

Monthly Journal Tabs: Make a copy of this page for each child. Direct the child to cut out the journal tab for the current month, fold it along the thin line, and glue it to the first blank page in his journal. Have him repeat the steps at the beginning of each new month.

Name _____

Month _____

What I've Read

Tips for Growing Carrots

Date	Title	Author	Minutes I Read

Daily Reading Prompts • ©The Mailbox® Books • TEC61269

Reading Log: Give each child a copy of this page and have him keep it in his reading journal. Each day, encourage the child to record his information on the chart.

Name _____

Title _____

Author _____

Book Review

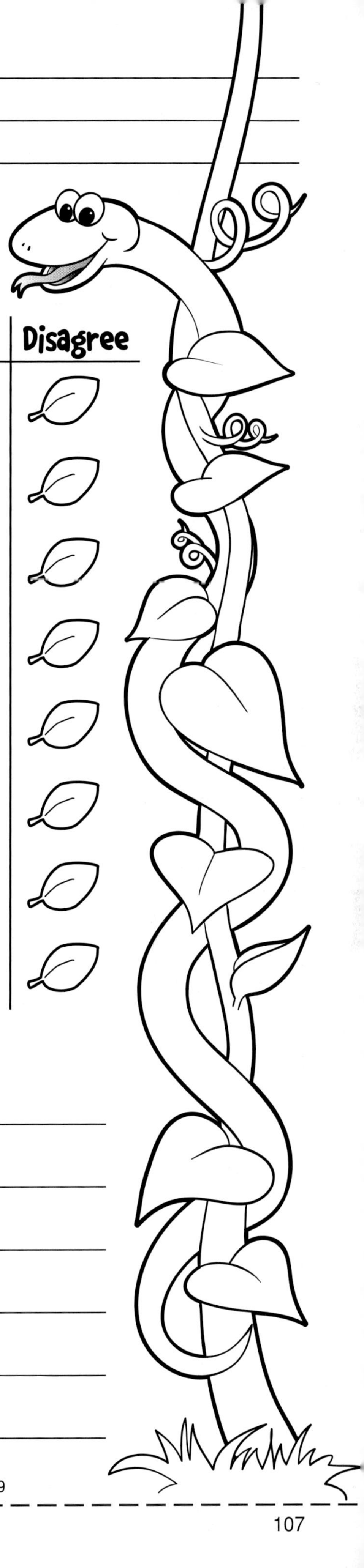

Color the leaf in the matching column.

	Agree	Disagree
1. I enjoyed this book.	🍃	🍃
2. I thought the problem was interesting.	🍃	🍃
3. I would have solved the problem the way the author did.	🍃	🍃
4. I would read another book by this author.	🍃	🍃
5. I liked the main character.	🍃	🍃
6. I would like to meet the main character.	🍃	🍃
7. I would read more books about this character.	🍃	🍃
8. I would like to visit the story's setting.	🍃	🍃

Comments

_____

_____

_____

_____

_____

Name _____

What I Can't Wait to Read

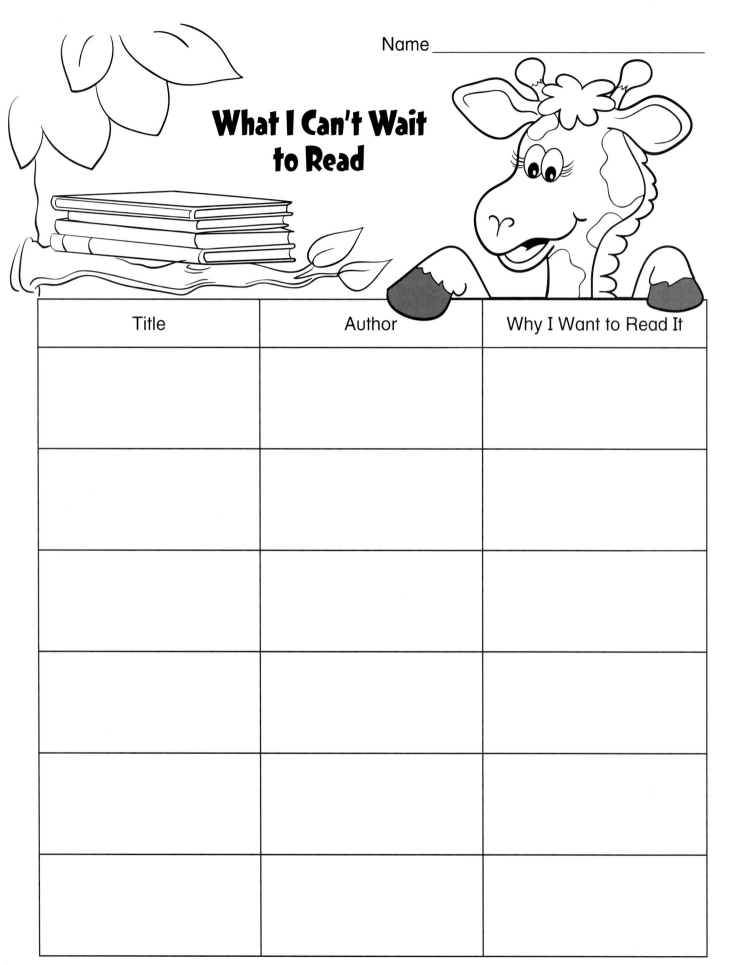

Title	Author	Why I Want to Read It

Reading Wish List: Give each child a copy of this page and have her keep it in her reading journal. Encourage the child to use the chart to keep track of books she would like to read.

What's This Word?

1. Look at the word.

2. Look in the word for parts you know.

3. Look at the first part of the word. Look at the last part of the word.

4. Read the words around it. What makes sense?

5. Ask.

TEC61269

---

name

Key Words From My Reading

TEC61269

Name _____

I wonder _____

_____

_____

_____

(Fold.)

I wonder _____

_____

_____

_____

TEC61269

Daily Reading Prompts • ©The Mailbox® Books • TEC61269

Bookmarks: Give a child a copy of each bookmark, as desired. Have the child use the top bookmark to help him decode unknown words, the middle bookmark to record vocabulary words, and the bottom bookmark to record questions and thoughts he has as he reads.

Name _____

Title _____

Telling the Story

Beginning

Middle

End

Daily Reading Prompts • ©The Mailbox® Books • TEC61269

110　**Story Map:** Use with any fictional story or biography.

Name _____

In Full Bloom

A Picture of the Character

Words That Describe the Character's Personality or Attitude

What the Character Looks Like

character's name

Character Web: Use with any fictional story or biography.

Name _____

To the Top!

Topic: _____

What I Know

What I Want to Know

What I Learned

112

KWL Chart: Use with any nonfiction or biography text.